Slide and Slurp, Scratch and Burp

Scratch and Burp

More about Verbs

To Isabella
—B.P.C.

Verb: A word that shows action or being

Slide and Slurp, Scratch and Burp

More about Verbs

by Brian P Cleary

illustrated by Brian Gable

LERNER BOOKS · LONDON · NEW YORK · MINNEAPOLIS

Verbs are words like
sneak and sniff,

sneeze and seize

and wheeze and whiff.

4

Planting carrots, getting traction,

Verbs give sentences their action.

You might be exploring
the Alps or the Amazon,
maybe restoring
the chair that your grandma's on,

knitting or hitting
or roping or biting—

Verbs can make sentences
very exciting.

They tell us of horses

that nuzzle and nip,

of bears as they guzzle

and birds as they sip.

They tell us of scooters
both swerving
and stopping,

throws that are curving
or sliding or dropping.

So wrap a package, tie a knot,
clap your hands, or cry a lot.

Triumph, tremble,

trot, and trample,

you'll use a **verb**
for each example!

Fly to the flower shop,
dash to the dance,

swing by the swimming pool,

frolic in France.

Soar to the circus and float to the fair.

Without verbs, your sentence can't go anywhere.

Each sentence **has** a subject—
it's just like the star.

It's what the whole thing's all about:

Dave's dish,

Mum's look,

Todd's car.

Subjects always need a Verb—

it's what makes fishes swim

and lanterns light
and writers write
and clippers cut and trim.

Some Verbs aren't the action kind—
They "link" instead of "do,"

connecting sentence parts, as in,
"Your dog appears quite blue."

These linking Verbs
connect a subject
to a Word or phrase

that's called a
Subject complement.
It's done in lots of Ways:

It became ridiculous.

That strudel smells so great.

The crime **remains** a mystery.

This play **seems** second rate.

The forms of "be"
are linking verbs,

like, "Are your names Michelle?"

Were and Was
Work this way, too—
they're forms of "be" as well.

I am Shannon.
He **is** Mort.

Were you the one
who was in court?

There **are** times
a form of "be"
is all that's **needed**, verbally.

25

Whether you slide

or you slip,

if you should scream

or you slurp,

or you scratch

or you burp,

if you're **making** a fraction
or **Writing** a blurb,

because there **is** action,
you **know** it's a verb.

So if you should gloat

or you glisten

or listen,

say to the chef,
"Take that out and put this in,"

Whether you pounce

or pronounce

or perturb,

I'm here to announce
that you're using a verb!

So, What IS a Verb?

Do you know?

ABOUT THE AUTHOR & ILLUSTRATOR

Brian P Cleary is the author of the best-selling Words Are CATegorical® series, as well as the Math Is CATegorical®, Sounds Like Reading™, and Adventures in Memory™ series, The Laugh Stand: Adventures in Humor, Peanut Butter and Jellyfishes: A Very Silly Alphabet Book, Rainbow Soup: Adventures in Poetry, and Rhyme & PUNishment: Adventures in Wordplay. Mr. Cleary lives in Cleveland, Ohio, USA.

Brian Gable is the illustrator of several Words Are CATegorical® books, as well as the Math Is CATegorical® series. Mr. Gable also works as a political cartoonist for the Globe and Mail newspaper in Toronto, Canada.

Text copyright © 2007 by Brian P. Cleary
Illustrations copyright © 2007 by Lerner Publishing Group, Inc.

First published in the United States of America in 2007

First published in the United Kingdom in 2010 by
Lerner Books,
Dalton House,
60 Windsor Avenue,
London SW19 2RR

Website address: www.lernerbooks.co.uk

British Library Cataloguing in Publication Data

Cleary, Brian P., 1959-
    Slide and slurp, scratch and burp : more about verbs.
    1. English language—Verb—Juvenile poetry.
    I. Title
    425.6—dc22

ISBN-13: 978 0 7613 5402 4

Printed in China